LEAN BELLY BREAKTHROUGH DIET
Lose Fat Program Book

By Dr David Shultz

ALL COPYRIGHTS RESERVED

Copyright 2017 by dr. David Shultz - All rights reserved.

This document is geared towards providing exact and reliable information in regards to the topic and issue covered. The publication is sold with the idea that the publisher is not required to render accounting, officially permitted, or otherwise, qualified services. If advice is necessary, legal or professional, a practiced individual in the profession should be ordered.

- From a Declaration of Principles which was accepted and approved equally by a Committee of the American Bar Association and a Committee of Publishers and Associations.

In no way is it legal to reproduce, duplicate, or transmit any part of this document in either electronic means or in printed format. Recording of this publication is strictly prohibited and any storage of this document is not allowed unless with written permission from the publisher. All rights reserved.

The information provided herein is stated to be truthful and consistent, in that any liability, in terms of inattention or otherwise, by any usage or abuse of any policies, processes, or directions contained within is the solitary and utter responsibility of the recipient reader. Under no circumstances will any legal responsibility or blame be held against the publisher for any reparation, damages, or monetary loss due to the information herein, either directly or indirectly.

Respective authors own all copyrights not held by the publisher.

The information herein is offered for informational purposes solely, and is universal as so. The presentation of the information is without contract or any type of guarantee assurance.

The trademarks that are used are without any consent, and the publication of the trademark is without permission or backing by the trademark owner. All trademarks and brands within this book are for clarifying purposes only and are the owned by the owners themselves, not affiliated with this document.

PREFACE

Why is it EASY to burn belly fat? If it were so easy, would not everyone be able to do it? Well, everyone is able to do it. Take a look at the amazing transformation stories you see in magazines. They are just everyday people like you and I...the only difference is the commitment they made to the advanced fat loss tips.

Fat loss is easy once you realize how hard it is. Once you understand that you can't get the body of your dreams from walking an extra flight of stairs each day, you'll realize that you have to get serious about your nutrition and strength and interval workouts. Once you do that, the fat will come off fast!

If you want advanced results, you must use advanced fat loss methods. End of story. There are no magic pills or potions. Follow all the guides illusrtates in the book,and you can start to lose fat without any stress.

Contents

LEAN BELLY BREAKTHROUGH DIET 1
   Lose Fat Program Book 1
ALL COPYRIGHTS RESERVED 2
PREFACE 3
CHAPTER 1-WHAT IS BODY FAT-THE EFFECT ON OUR BODY 4
CHAPTER 2- FAT LOSS AND DIET-THE BEST DIET TO LOSE FAT 8
CHAPTER 3- NATURAL FAT-LOSS REMEDY 11
CHAPTER 4- ALCOHOL AND FAT LOSS 25
CHAPTER 5- MISTAKES THAT SABOTAGE FAT LOSS 28
CHAPTER 6- STRATEGIES FOR ENHANCING FAT LOSS 30
   CHAPTER 7- WHAT ARE GOOD FATS- LIST OF LOW-FAT FOODS 44
CHAPTER 8- BODY FAT SCALE- HOW TO MEASURE THE BODY FAT 53
CHAPTER 9- HOW TO REMOVE STOMACH FAT 56
CHAPTER 10- CONCLUSION 69

CHAPTER 1-WHAT IS BODY FAT-THE EFFECT ON OUR BODY

The term 'body fat' is a familiar one. However, most people associate this word to obesity, cholesterol and an unhealthy constitution. Although excess body fat content can have severe implications, the body requires a specific content of body fat for various metabolic and structural functions.

Body fat is produced in the body through the absorption of fats present in the food consumed. As the body breaks down these fats, two byproducts are released into the body – glycerol and fatty acids. The liver processes glycerol into glucose and stores it as a stock of energy. Fatty acids provide energy for all major tissues, especially for the cardiac muscles and the skeletal muscles. So, it is very important to include appropriate amounts of fatty substances in the diet.

Here are few major functions of body fats:

Body fats help to maintain healthy skin and hair.

To maintain the right body temperature, it is essential to have adequate body fat. • Body fats are the storehouses of energy in the body.

Body fats are necessary to ensure the smooth functioning of cells.

Body fats have a cushioning effect on organs and tissues.

Body fats act as a shock absorber for bones.

The body will not be able to absorb many vital vitamins like A, E, D and K unless they are able to combine with fats.

Body fats are also believed to act as immunity boosters to protect the body from ailments.

Too Much Body Fat – Why Is It Undesirable?

Although the body cannot function smoothly without body fat, it is also important to remember that too much of body fat can negatively affect the body. Very often, the fats absorbed by the body do not burn off but get stored in the body. Such accumulation of body fats may lead to obesity that can then set off many other health issues like breathing difficulties, arthritis, and heart disease.

To prevent problems associated with too much body fat, one must be aware of the current body fat percentage in the body and the ideal percentage required. According to the American Council on Exercise, body fat must ideally constitute 14 – 17 percentage of the total weight of a man. In the case of women, body fat must be around 21 – 24 percentage of total weight.

Knowing the exact fat percentage in your body can help in setting realistic weight loss plans. With the various fat measurement techniques available today, it is very easy to keep track of the body fat and adopt steps to a healthy lifestyle. Four popular fat measurement methods are Home Body Fat Scales, Navy Method, Hydrostatic Weighing and Skinfold Calipers.

How Does Body Fat Loss Differ From Weight Loss?

Body fat loss and weight loss are two completely different concepts. Consider an instance of two individuals belonging to the same age group – an athletically built person and a normal person. Due to the extra weight of muscles, the athletic person may weigh more than his counterpart. However, the second person's weight may be related to a higher content of body fat. Obviously, this person will be more vulnerable to weight-related issues than the athletic person. Therefore, it is important to lose body fat rather than trying to lose body weight. With new methods that measure body fat percentage, you can get a accurate report of your body fat and the amount you must lose or gain to remain fit and healthy.

When trying weight loss plans to lose body fat, it is best to adopt a plan that combines a good exercise regimen with a healthy diet of fresh fruits, vegetables, whole grains and a minimum of processed carbohydrates. You should keep the body fat levels to the ideal percentage and enjoy more health and happiness in your life.

CHAPTER 2- FAT LOSS AND DIET-THE BEST DIET TO LOSE FAT

What is diet

Does the word "diet" immediately make you think of an unpleasant weight-loss regimen?

If it did, you are probably not alone. For example, consider the use of the term "diet" in marketing food products—it usually describes foods low in calories, such as diet soda.

But there is another meaning of this word. Diet can also refer to the food and drink a person consumes daily and the mental and physical circumstances connected to eating. Nutrition involves more than simply eating a "good" diet—it is about nourishment on every level. It involves relationships with family, friends, nature (the environment), our bodies, our community, and the world.

An unhealthy diet is one of the major risk factors for a range of chronic diseases, including cardiovascular diseases, cancer, diabetes and other conditions linked to obesity. Specific recommendations for a healthy diet include eating more fruit, vegetables, legumes, nuts,and grains; cutting down on salt, sugar and fats. It is also advisable to choose unsaturated fats, instead of saturated fats and towards the elimination of trans-fatty acids.

If you're sick and tired of having that extra fat around your middle, there are diets that can help you lose belly fat very fast - some of it at least. These diets have been proven to work, and if you keep eating this way for life, you will have a very healthy eating plan that is good for your heart and health.

What is the best diet for belly fat?

Of course, you want to use the most effective eating plan that works if you're wondering what is the best diet for belly fat? All of the plans that work have some things in common. They tell you to not eat sugar or processed foods that are made with sugar. Basic natural foods are allowed, including lean meat, vegetables, fruits, and whole grains. All of these plans encourage eating in moderation and not overdoing it on any one particular food, so a balanced diet is the key to losing that stubborn midsection weight. Dietitians and nutritionists have looked at Mediterranean countries and France where people eat meat, cheese, bread, and other foods that we love, but they don't gain weight. They believe that the olive oil that is in their diet is the secret to the reason why they stay slim. Almost every best diet for belly fat loss includes this oil.

Any version of the Mediterranean diet is the best diet for belly fat loss

A best diet for belly fat loss is almost always a lot like the Mediterranean eating plan. There is a Mediterranean food pyramid that includes a great variety of fruits, vegetables, beans, nuts, legumes, herbs, spices, and bread on the bottom which means that these foods should be eaten the most. Olive oil is included in this category and next up is the fish bracket. Poultry and eggs are next, and the top consists of meats and sweets - they should be the least amount of food eaten. Wine and water should also be part of the daily food plan. Eating like this will help you lose belly fat in a week, and you will keep losing it as you continue to eat these foods. Snacks and dessert are almost always fruit. This diet emphasizes the importance of eating meals with others and enjoying the food that you eat.

Best eating plan for losing the spare tire

So what is the best diet for belly fat? It's any eating plan that focuses on eating red meat no more than once a week, and focusing on eating whole grains, fruits, vegetables, nuts, seeds, and olive oil. Lean poultry and fish can be eaten on other days, but there should be some meatless meals as well. If you prefer to have meal plans with meals already set so that all you need to do is follow it, then the Flat Belly plan is for you. It has 28 interchangeable meals that can be mixed and matched. It also gives you 80 recipes that will help you drop the pounds. Another plan that works is The Cinch eating plan that allows you to eat four meals each day and a small piece of dark chocolate every day. Some of the meals on this plan should be vegetarian in order to lose fat.

CHAPTER 3- NATURAL FAT-LOSS REMEDY

Every other person on this planet wants to lose belly fat! Yes it is this great an issue. Belly fat not only gives you an ugly look but can be dangerous for your health too. The visceral fat or the fat around your abdomen can lead to diabetes, heart diseases, stroke as well as dementia. When it comes to lose abdominal fat, the right foods are a necessity. They detox your liver and boost your metabolism so that your body can target belly fat. There are numerous fat burning foods and spices that can help you lose your belly fat. Here are some really effective home remedies to lose belly fat with the help of such foods and spices.

How to Lose Belly Fat with Natural Remedies

1. Drink Lemon Water to Lose Belly Fat

You need to detoxify your liver because a stressed liver cannot metabolize fat effectively and which gets deposited around your waistline. Lemon water excellently increases enzymes that detoxify your liver so that it may carry out its basic functions efficiently.

Get this:

Lemon- 1

Water (warm preferred)- 1 glass

Do this:

After you get up in the morning, take the lemon and squeeze out its juice into the water.

While warm water is good to make lemon water for fat burning purpose, you can also use water at room temperature. This won't stop lemon doing its job.

Mix well and drink this lemon water on an empty stomach every day in the morning.

Do not eat or drink anything for at least 30 minutes after you have your regular lemon water every morning.

2. Drink Cranberry Juice to Lose Belly Fat

Cranberries are a rich source of organic acids like malic acid, citric acid, and quinic acid that function as digestive enzymes. These acids act as emulsifying agents on stubborn fat deposits in your lymphatic system which transports all the waste products that your liver cannot process. Cranberry juice digests these lymphatic wastes and help you reduce fat. So, drink 100 percent cranberry juice (unsweetened) or cran-water.

Get this:

Unsweetened cranberry juice- 8 oz. Or 1 cup

Water- 56 oz. Or 7 cup

Do this:

In the morning, mix cranberry juice with water to get your day's supply of cran-water.

Have one cup of this cran-water at a time through out the day.

You may have a cup each before breakfast and lunch, after dinner, and at other times of the day.

You may also make this cran-water just before you have it. Just mix 2 tablespoons of cranberry juice to 7 oz. (a little less than a cup) of plain water.

Fish Oil or Fish to Lose Belly Fat

3. Have Fish Oil or Fish to Lose Belly Fat

Fish oil has omega-3 fatty acids in it. Omega 3 acids such as icosapentaenoic acid, docosahexaenoic acid and linolenic acid help in breaking down fat while reducing fat storage around your waistline. If you can't take fish oil, have fish rich in omega 3 fatty acids.

Do this

Have 6 g of fish oil daily. 6 g roughly equals a generously filled tablespoon which is on the verge of overflowing.

Alternatively, you may have such fish as salmon or mackerel two times a week. Tuna and halibut are also high on omega-3.

4. Eat Chia Seeds to Lose Belly Fat

If you are a vegan and cannot have fish to get your day's dose of omega 3 fatty acids, you can eat chia seeds that are equally high on omega-3 and are best plant based source of omega 3 acids. However, your body needs to work a little to convert the alpha- linolenic acid in these seeds into DHA or EPA that directly comes from fish oil. Apart from omega 3 acids, chia seeds are good source of antioxidants, calcium, iron and dietary fiber which helps you feel fuller for longer. The diet book, 'The Aztec Diet' suggests having 4-8 tbsp (1-2 oz or 30-

60 g) of chia seeds during a day to keep you less hungry and prevent you from overeating. However, 1 tablespoon of chia seeds too is a good amount to include in your daily diet

How to eat chia seeds?

Add chia seeds to your smoothies, salads and yogurt.

Add them to your breakfast cereal.

Use chia seeds as a thickening agent for soups and gravies.

5. Have Ginger Tea to Lose Belly fat

You know that ginger is a natural digestive aid but did you know that ginger is a thermogenic? Thermogenic agents increase body temperature thus helping burn fat more effectively. Your belly fat may be due to one of the various reasons like overeating, age-related reduction of hormone, lack of exercise or stress. Ginger can practically solve each of these issues. Ginger is also said to suppress cortisol production. Cortisol is a steroid hormone essential for energy regulation and mobilization. So, have ginger tea daily to aid your efforts of losing belly fat.

How to make ginger lemon honey tea?

Get this:

Water- 4 cups

Ginger (peeled and sliced)- 1-2 inch piece

Lemon- 1

Honey- 1 tbsp

Do this:

Boil the water.

Add ginger to the hot water and simmer for 5-10 minutes.

Remove from the stove and add lemon juice and honey to this.

Mix well and have a cup of this ginger tea in the morning.

To regulate your metabolism, stimulate your digestion and reduce your cortisol production, have at least 2 cups of ginger tea throughout the day.

6. Use Garlic to Lose Belly Fat

You might be knowing that garlic is good for your cardiovascular system as it reduces both systolic and diastolic blood pressure as well as triglycerides apart from increasing good cholesterol. You might, however, not be knowing that garlic has excellent anti-obesity properties too! Every minute our body cells die and our body makes new cells to replace them. Adipocytes (also called lipocytes and fat cells) are the cells in our body which primarily compose adipose tissue (body fat). In the adipose tissue, there undergoes a process wherein pre-adipocytes are converted into full-fledged adipose tissue or fat. This process is known as adipogenesis. Studies show that garlic inhibits this process of adipogenisis or the process of making fat. If stated in simple language, garlic stops your pre fat cells from converting into fat cells. So, you might well like to add garlic into your daily diet. However, raw garlic is more beneficial when you want to lose belly fat!

Get this:

Garlic cloves- 3

Lemon- 1

Water- 1 cup

Do this:

Squeeze the lemon juice into the cup of water.

Chew 3 garlic cloves and then drink the lemon water

Repeat every morning on a empty stomach.

You will start losing belly fat within 2 week's time.

7. Herbs Infused Water to Lose Belly Fat

There are many herbs in your kitchen that you don't even call herbs. You use them daily in your cooking or in salads etc. but you are unaware of there effects on your body fat. Some of such herbs includes ginger, mint, and cucumber. These herbs, when combined with the excellent fat burner lemon can do wonders to get you rid of belly fat. Consisting of water and dietary fiber, cucumber is a great food to lose belly fat. It cleanses your body from deep within and helps you lose weight. Ginger is a great fat burner which allows blood vessels to expand leading to better blood circulation. It also boosts metabolism. A study suggests that people who eat ginger can lose 20% more weight than people who don't eat it. Due to its rich contents of vitamin C and antioxidants, lemon boosts your energy apart from burning fat. Mint not only calms down your cravings but also soothes tummy after you indulge in foods. Water keeps you hydrated and this flavored water will also detoxify your body. So, here's the recipe of what you might call a flat belly diet drink.

Get this:

Water- 2 liters

Cucumber (sliced)- 1 medium

Ginger (grated or pressed)- 1 tsp if grated; 1-2 inch piece if pressed

Lemon (sliced)- 1

Mint leaves- 10-12 sprigs

Do this:

Soak all the ingredients in water overnight.

Once they are infused for the whole night, drink this water throughout the day.

8. Dandelion Tea to Lose Belly Fat

If your belly fat is due to water retention, dandelion herb can come to your rescue. Dandelion is a natural diuretic which increase your urine output. Dandelion will improve your liver's functioning capacity. It will flush out retained water and toxins out of your body, especially from belly area which you know by the name of abdominal bloating. Combined with some fat reducing spices, dandelion tea not only tastes good but helps reduce belly fat which is due to water retention.

Get this:

Dandelion root (roasted)- 1 tbsp OR Dandelion root powder (roasted)- 1 tsp

Fresh ginger (minced)- half an inch piece

Cardamom seeds- from 1 cardamom

Cinnamon bark- half inch piece

Mint leaves- 4-5

Water- 1 and ½ cup

Honey (optional)- 1-2 tsp as per taste

Do this:

Add all the ingredients except honey to water.

Bring this water to a boil.

Boil the water for 5-10 minutes

Strain the tea and add honey to this if using.

Mix well and have this delicious dandelion root tea.

You may have 2-4 cups of this tea during the day.

Precaution: If you have blocked bile ducts or some issues related to gall bladder, avoid having dandelion tea. Consult your doctor before taking this tea.

9. Have Cinnamon to Lose Belly Fat

Don't go by the sweet taste of cinnamon, it won't increase your fat. In fact, cinnamon will help reduce your overall body fat including the belly fat. Cinnamon is a thermogenic. It means, cinnamon tends to produce heat through metabolic stimulation. Thus cinnamon makes you burn your fat. So, include 1 tsp. of ground cinnamon to your daily diet in order to increase your metabolism. Take ground cinnamon and not the cinnamon bark oil which may lead to ulcers, mouth sores and mouth burning when consumed. Cinnamon is one spice that you can cook with any food.

Ways to have cinnamon to loose belly fat

Sprinkle a tsp of cinnamon on top of your beverages like tea, coffee or even milk.

Add cinnamon on top of your toast, muffin etc.

Add cinnamon powder to your breakfast cereal.

Sprinkle it on your salad, dips, and sauces.

10. Lean Meat to Burn Fat and Lose Belly Fat

Foods that have thermogenic properties burn your calories as you eat them. Protein is highly thermogenic. Animal proteins are more thermogenic than vegetable proteins. Thus, lean meats are the best calorie burning food. When you eat lean meat, you burn about 30 percent of the calories it contains within it just by digesting the food. So, if you eat a 300 calorie chicken breast, you will use about 90 calories to digest it. It's wise to include some protein in each of your meal. This can be lean chicken, beef, or pork, especially in dinner so that you burn most of the consumed calories through digestion at a time when your body's metabolism is slower. Just remember, do not fry your lean meat!

11. Sip Green Tea to Lose Belly Fat

The American Journal of Clinical Nutrition states, having 4 cups of green tea daily helped people lose more than six pounds within a period of eight weeks. Green tea contains a type of a catechin called epigallocatechin-3-gallate, or EGCG. It is a natural phenol and antioxidant with many therapeutic applications. When you sip green tea, EGCG in it boosts your metabolism. Have 3-4 cups of green tea daily. Make it fresh every time or store it in the fridge to get an iced green tea each time you need to speed up your metabolism. Here is a fine recipe of fat burning green tea for you.

How to make green tea to lose belly fat?

Get this:

Green tea leaves or pearls- 1-2 tsp OR Green tea bag- 1

Hot water- 1 cup

Mint/basil leaves- 4-5

Lemon juice- ½ to 1 tsp

Honey (optional)- 1-2 tsp as per taste

Do this:

Add green tea (or tea bag) and mint or basil leaves to the hot water.

Cover and steep for 5-10 minutes.

Strain and add lemon juice plus honey if using.

Mix well and sip your green tea.

Have three to four cups of green tea daily, preferably after meals.

12. Hot Peppers to Lose Belly Fat

Hot peppers contain capsaicin which has thermogenic effects. It boosts your body's heat production and thus uses more energy or calorie. A study published in the "American Journal of Clinical Nutrition" says that when capsaicinoids are consumed daily, it reduces abdominal fat and improves fat oxidation. So spice up your foods with hot peppers to lose belly fat. Eat peppers raw, cooked, dried, or in powdered form. Red peppers contain different amounts of capsaicin, making some peppers more hot than others. Habanero pepper has the highest amount of capsaicin but cayenne pepper too can be a good choice. Although not as hot, cayenne pepper do has a significant amount of capsaicin which can increase fat burning and lead to your belly fat loss. Don't be shy to add as much cayenne or hot sauce as you can to your soups, eggs, gravies and meats.

13. Coconut Oil to Lose Belly Fat

Don't be surprised. Although it is a fat, coconut oil can actually help lose your belly fat! I'll tell you how. This oil extracted from coconut has a unique combination of fatty acids. It has a positive effect on your metabolism too. Coconut oil is high on medium chain triglycerides. The medium chain fatty acids are metabolized differently from long chain fatty acids. These fatty acids directly go to the liver from your digestive tract, where they are used in one of the two ways- either as energy or are converted into ketone bodies. Ketone bodies are three water-soluble biochemical compounds that are produced by the liver using fatty acids when you fast or reduce your food intake. These are used by body cells as energy instead of glucose. So when you want to follow low carb diet to lose fat, coconut oil can help you alot.

Coconut oil is also a thermogenic and burns fat. Many studies have shown that medium chain fatty acids when compared to the similar amount of calories from other fats, can improve feeling of fullness. Thus you automatically reduce calorie intake.

A study has shown positive results about coconut oil in reducing abdominal fat. In this study, some women were given 2 tablespoons of coconut oil and some other women were given 2 tablespoons of soybean oil for 28 days. Both the groups lost about 2 pounds but the group taking coconut oil also reduced their waist circumference while those on soybean oil had a mild increase in belly fat. The coconut oil group also increased HDL (good) cholesterol levels. However, mindlessly having coconut oil may in fact increase your weight, after all it is a fat. So, keep the following tips in mind when using coconut oil to lose belly fat.

Tips to use coconut oil to lose belly fat

Do not add coconut oil to the existing oils that you use daily. You must replace other cooking oil with coconut oil.

Do not have loads of coconut oil. Just 2 tablespoons a day is sufficient.

Remember, coconut oil is to aid your efforts for losing fat. Your primary diet should always be whole, nutritious foods.

14. Easy Lifestyle Changes to Lose Belly Fat

Sometimes you exercise adequately and adopt a host of natural remedies to lose belly fat but still, you can't. If that's what happening with you, you need to analyze your lifestyle and make some small changes. These changes are very small but may need a while to convert into a habit. If you really want to get rid of your abdominal fat, you better start bringing these lifestyle changes from now itself.

Sleep adequately- Lack of sleep is one of the prominent causes for belly fat accumulation. When you don't sleep, you crave for sugar and fatty foods. It also spikes your cortisol hormone which makes you insensitive to insulin. As a result, you lose your body's bio-rhythm. So, sleep well.

Reduce or stop alcohol consumption- Alcohol is full of calories but when you consume alcohol you don't feel full. Binge drinking in particular deposits fat around your waistline. It's better not to have alcohol but if you can't do that at least avoid binge drinking and also reduce the quantity and frequency of alcohol intake.

15. Develop Right Food Habits to Lose Belly Fat

Yes food can get you rid of belly fat if you are eating the right food though. Here's how you can develop good food habit and lose your belly fat.

Choose snacks intelligently- What you call light snacks do more harm. Burgers, pizzas, French fries and all that junk food is not good for your body. Eat less of them as also sodas and processed foods. Foods indicating low calorie, low fat or sugar-free too can contribute to belly fat. Artificial sweeteners in these foods may induce your body to store fat. Avoid them and opt for healthy snacks like fruits, nuts etc.

Reduce sugar in your diet- Sugar is one of the main causes of fat. Instead of sugar, have complex carbohydrates. Your body converts complex carbohydrates into sugar and they are beneficial for you.

Have more good food- eat more of protein, vegetables, fresh raw fruits, whole grains and nuts. Remember canned fruits and veggies can further increase your belly fat so avoid them.

Have more of good fat- Omega 3 fats help lose belly fat. So have more of foods having this good fat such as salmon. Low glycemic-index foods such as beans too are beneficial when it comes to losing belly fat.

Consume more vitamin C- It must come from natural sources like lemon, orange, kiwi fruit etc.

Don't skip meals- When you starve your body, it gets into survival mode and starts storing foods in the form of fat. So, have your breakfast, lunch and dinner daily. Keep your meals small and snack on healthy foods in between these main meals.

16. Exercise to Lose Belly Fat

Yes, you cannot spare this. You must exercise too. All the natural remedies to lose belly fat and good food and lifestyle habits will go waste if you don't exercise. This is the eternal truth. The fast you understand this, the early you will lose your belly fat!

Do whole body workouts- Losing belly fat just by spot exercising stomach won't do. Exercise your entire muscle groups in whole body workouts.

Do cardiovascular exercises- Walking, jogging, running, cycling, aerobics etc. increases your body's capacity to burn more calories.

Do Strength training- Along with cardiovascular exercising, do strength training too. It will build your muscle tone to help you get rid of overall body fat

CHAPTER 4- ALCOHOL AND FAT LOSS

Can I drink Alcohol while I'm trying to lose weight?"

or

"How much Alcohol is it OK to drink while I'm trying to lose weight?"

This is a common question that many people have when trying to lose weight.

And in many cases we want to "have our cake and eat it too."

Right?

I mean, there is really nothing wrong with that but when you're trying to make progress it's important that you recognize the facts when it comes to how alcohol effects your fat loss efforts.

Now here's the bottom line: one or two drinks a couple of nights a week is not going to stop you from making progress.

But if you are very serious about making progress I would ask you to consider why you even want to partake in that.

For example, if I was coaching you personally and you came to me and said that you want to make maximum progress in minimum time then I would suggest you limit drinking to once a week. (or zero if you can manage that.)

Here's why:

1) Alcohol is loaded with empty calories. These are carbohydrates that are ultimately going to turn into fat.

You might see some advertisement for some "ultra-light" beers with only 99 calories. Well, that's still 99 calories!

Drink 2 or 3 and you just put 200-300 empty calories in your body.

2) Alcohol sparks your appetite and makes you crave the foods you should not be eating.

OK, let's say you decide to have a glass of wine with dinner. On paper, this is no big deal. But in REALITY what actually happens?

First of all this makes you hungrier and you may begin to have serious cravings for foods you should not be eating like processed carbohydrates (pasta, french fries) Personally, when I consume alcohol I crave fast food. Come to think of it, I crave anything!

3) Alcohol DESTROYS your momentum.

This is really the worst part. If you want to breakthrough fat loss plateau then momentum is absolutely critical. If you want to stop yourself from ever getting momentum then by all means drink regularly.

Let's be honest: what normally happens when you drink Alcohol and end up overeating?

Do you feel on track the next day? Personally, I've noticed the effects last through the next day. So the point is to see the total outcome that drinking will have.

Now keep in mind that I'm writing this book to help you lose maximum fat in minimum time. Once you achieve your goals then you can figure out "what you can get away with." As far as I'm concerned there's nothing wrong with that.

For the time being try this: one night a week drink as much as you want. One drink, 3 drinks, five drinks, whatever (as long as you are safe).

So if you drink on a Saturday night then you can simply relax on Sunday and it might even be a great time to give yourself some leeway in your diet. Enjoy yourself Saturday night and most of the day Sunday.

If this sounds too "extreme" for you and you can't go without drinking most nights that's fine, you can still make progress but you want come anywhere close to the progress you could make.

Ask yourself, "How much do I really want to lose fat?" "How much do I want to drink every night of the week"

The answers could be very telling.

CHAPTER 5- MISTAKES THAT SABOTAGE FAT LOSS

The good news is that extreme fat loss can happen for you, but the bad news is that if you are committing one or more of these 6 deadly mistakes, then your chances of getting in shape is very minimal.

Mistake #1 - Not Putting Your Primary Attention On Nutrition - Nothing will EVER work if your primary focus is not on getting proper nutrition. Exercising, diet pills, supplements, etc. can't hold a flame to the effects you could receive from getting 100% proper nutrition. If you place most of your attention on nutrition, then you will start to notice immediate results, and you certainly will get the body you want much more easier.

Mistake #2 - Not Eating Enough Raw Fruits, Nuts, And Veggies - Raw foods will speed up your metabolism, burn off fat just from eating them, enhance your digestive system, and more. Not getting enough raw foods in your diet will do the exact opposite of everything I just mentioned!

Mistake #3 - You're Not Eating Enough Healthy Fats - Monounsaturated, polyunsaturated, and omega fatty acids are all important to include in your diet. Not getting enough of these nutrients will decrease your fat burning and muscle-building hormones.

Mistake #4 - Not Drinking Enough Water - Besides not getting proper nutrition, not drinking enough water is right up there with being the number one reason people can't burn fat or lose weight. When you don't drink enough water, your body will retain water, and this will add on SEVERAL pounds. Also, when you don't drink enough water, your metabolism will decrease, your digestive system is sabotaged, your energy levels will decrease, and so much more!

Mistake #5 - Too Much Cardio, Not Enough Muscle Building - Aerobic exercising is absolutely fine, but if you are doing too much of it and at the same time not doing enough muscle-building workouts, then you are seriously inhibiting your ability to burn fat effectively. This is because building lean muscle is actually more important than cardio, and this is because muscle tissue itself burns off calories... and when you don't have enough it, then it's inevitable that you're going to reach a plateau!

Mistake #6 - Your Making Your Metabolism Slower Instead Of Boosting It - Fad dieting, taking diet pills, committing one of those 5 mistakes above, not getting enough sleep, skipping breakfast, and eating too late are things that can cause your metabolism to slow down. If this happens, then losing weight will be EXTREMELY difficult.

CHAPTER 6- STRATEGIES FOR ENHANCING FAT LOSS

With the worldwide obesity epidemic, many individuals are searching for ways to lose weight and keep it off. While the focus is often on total body weight, it is actually excess body fat that represents the real health threat. Thus it is important to understand the role that body fat plays in health and disease and how to achieve a healthy level of body fat.

Overweight or Obese

An individual's body weight or body composition reflects the level of lean body mass (tissue, bone, and muscle) and body fat. While the words obese and overweight are used synonymously there is a great difference between these terms in both efinition and associated health risk.

Overweight is defined as a body weight above an acceptable weight in relation to height. This term can be misleading because it does not distinguish between excess body fat and lean muscle mass. For example, it is possible to be overweight without being obese. A body-builder would be an example of this scenario. Having a greater proportion of muscle mass would make this individual appear overweight according to standard weight/height charts, yet this person could have low body fat and be in good physical shape.

Obesity is defined as having excess body fat in relation to lean body mass. By generally accepted standards, men with greater than 25 percent, and women with more than 30 percent body fat, are considered to be obese.

Since it is excess fat (not excess weight) that is a health concern, when assessing your overall fitness level it is important to look at the percentage of your body that is composed of fat, rather than just total body weight.

Factors Affecting Body Fat

There are many factors that regulate your level of body fat, including:

· Diet

· Activity level

· Basal metabolic rate (rate at which calories are burned at rest)

· Genetics

· Hormones, such as insulin, thyroid, and growth hormone

Body Fat Distribution - Apples versus Pears

Just as the degree of obesity is important in determining health risk, so is the location of the fat. The "apple" shaped body, which is defined by abdominal fatness or 'pot belly', has been found to predispose an individual to Type 2 diabetes, dyslipidemia, hypertension, coronary heart disease, stroke, and early mortality. In fact, waist circumference measurements have been shown to be a better predictor of health risk than the body mass index (BMI).

For men:

Increased risk - waist more than 94 cm (38 inches)

Substantially increased risk - waist more than 102 cm (40 inches)

For women:

Increased risk - waist more than 80 cm (32 inches)

Substantially increased risk - waist more than 88 cm (35 inches)

Men in particular often deposit weight in the waist region, whereas women tend to gain weight around the hips and buttocks giving them the "pear" shape." Fat deposited primarily around the hips and buttocks does not carry the same risk as that gained around the mid-section.

The tendency to deposit fat around the mid-section is influenced by a number of factors including genetics and lifestyle choices. Physical activity, avoiding smoking and using unsaturated fat over saturated fat have been shown to decrease the risk of developing abdominal obesity.

Recommended Levels of Body Fat

An individual's body fat is expressed as a percentage of body weight that is made up of fat. This percentage varies for men and for women and with age.

All of us require some stored body fat for fueling energy and cushioning. If the body has too little fat, it will begin to break down muscle tissue for energy requirements.

Below are recommended body fat ranges for women and men according to the American Dietetics Association:

Women

Normal 15-25 %

Overweight 25.1-29.9 %

Obese Over 30 %

Men

Normal 10-20 %

Overweight 20.1-24.4 %

Obese Over 25 %

Checking your Body Fat Level

Height and weight tables, such as the body mass index (BMI) are commonly used to determine how a person's weight compares to a standard. This method is easy to do since it involves simple measures of height and weight, yet because it does not distinguish between the proportions of body fat and lean tissue it is not the most accurate method of assessing one's health risk due to excess body fat.

Here are some methods that can be used to determine your body fat percentage:

Skin Fold Calipers - measures the thickness of subcutaneous fat at various locations on the body. The measurements obtained are used in special equations to obtain an estimated percent fat value. This method is not very accurate and is dependent upon the skills and judgment of the person performing the test

Bioelectric Impedance - a machine is used to measure an electric signal as it passes through lean body mass and fat. The higher the fat content the greater the resistance to the current. This method is more effective than skin fold caliper testing, but is not 100%.

Near Infrared Technology - infrared light is shined on to the skin (usually bicep area). Fat absorbs the light, while lean body mass reflects the lights back. The reflected light is measured by a special sensor, transmitted into the computer, and translated into percentage of body fat. This method is highly accurate - comparable to underwater weighing but slightly more expensive that the above two methods.

DEXA - stands for dual energy X-ray absorptiometry -uses two X-ray energies to measure body fat, muscle, and bone mineral. This method is highly accurate but also the mst expensive and time consuming.

Health Benefits of a Lean Body

Having a lean body is important for overall health and longevity. Our body composition impacts how we look and how we feel. When we are physically fit we feel better about ourselves, have more energy and enjoy better well being. Conversely, carrying excess fat can have a negative impact on our self-esteem, confidence, and body image. It can also cause fatigue and lethargy, making the simplest of tasks, such as going up a flight of stairs, difficult and exhausting.

Numerous studies have found that that who maintain a lean body live longer, suffer less disease and enjoy a better quality of life. It is important to know that even small losses can lead to great health rewards. Studies have found that losing even 10-15% of excess weight (fat) can help to reduce blood pressure, blood sugar, cholesterol and triglycerides.

Lifestyle Recommendations for a Lean Body

While nutritional supplements can be very helpful, healthy eating and regular physical exercise form the foundation of a successful, long-term weight management and fat loss program.

Below is some nutritional tips to consider for healthy fat loss:

· Eat at least three meals a day, preferably four to five small meals to keep your metabolism and energy level optimized. Do not skip meals as this can raise your appetite, deplete your energy levels and lead to binge eating.

· When you are hungry between meals, snack on healthful foods, such as fruit, yogurt, raw vegetables, nuts and seeds.

· Emphasize fresh, unprocessed foods. Low-fat/low calorie, nutrient-dense foods are your best dietary choices. These include fresh fruits, vegetables, legumes (beans, peas, and lentils) and whole grains. Cut down on processed and refined foods, such as fast food, junk food, white bread/rice/pasta, candy, cookies and sweets. Refined grains lack nutritional value because their outer fiber-rich layer is stripped away during the refinement. Processed food and junk food should be looked upon as providing "empty calories" because these foods are often high in sugar and calories but very low in nutritional value.

· Limit your intake of saturated and hydrogenated fats. Fat fills you up more slowly than other foods because it takes longer to metabolize and absorb from the gastrointestinal tract. The feeling of fullness (satiety) is delayed causing you to eat more. Less chewing is required, so these fatty foods are consumed quickly. Furthermore, fat is more calorie-dense, providing nine calories per gram, compared to only four calories per gram provided by protein and carbohydrates.

· Ensure adequate protein intake. Protein is essential for building and maintaining lean muscle mass. Without adequate protein intake, dieting, and exercise can cause the body to burn muscle for fuel and this can result in a lowering of your basal metabolic rate - the rate at which you burn calories. The recommended amount of protein is based on body weight and activity level. For the average person, this amount is 0.8 to 1 gram per kilogram, or one-half gram per pound of body weight.

· Fill up on fiber. Dietary fiber is a powerful asset to anyone trying to lose body fat. Dietary fiber helps balance blood sugar and insulin levels and improves digestion and elimination. Fiber also makes us feel more full with meals because it slows digestion. Most health agencies recommend 25 to 35 g of fiber per day. Plant foods, such as vegetables, fruit, whole grains and legumes, are excellent sources of natural fiber. Fiber is also available in supplemental form, such as powders and tablets.

· If you drink alcoholic beverages, do so in moderation. Alcohol floods the body with empty calories. Depending on the beverage, it provides anywhere from 20 to 124 calories per ounce.

· Cut down on salt and sodium. Most of the sodium in the typical diet comes from the saltshaker and processed foods. A high-sodium diet is unhealthy and causes fluid retention, meaning it can contribute to water weight gain.

Consistent exercise promotes the loss of body fat in several ways:

· Increased energy expenditure - Exercise or physical activity burns calories and stored fat.

· After burn - Your basal metabolic rate is heightened for four to 24 hours after vigorous physical activity, especially weight lifting or anaerobic exercise. Aerobic exercise, such as running or aerobics, typically boosts your metabolism for 60 minutes. It's important to combine both cardiovascular exercise, such as walking, running, biking and anaerobic exercise such as weight lifting to achieve and maintain optimum results, and more importantly, keep the results.

· Increased lean body mass - Exercise is critical for building and maintaining strong, healthy muscles and muscle burns more calories than any other part of the body. Increasing lean muscle mass helps the body to utilize fat more efficiently as fuel. Dieting without exercise can actually undermine your weight loss efforts by leading to loss of muscle mass along with fat. When this happens metabolism slows down and your burn less calories.

· Balancing blood sugar - Exercise pulls stored calories, or energy, in the forms of glucose and fat out of tissues. In this way, blood glucose levels stay balanced and you are less likely to feel hungry.

Nutritional Supplements to Aid Fat Loss

Healthy eating and exercise are the foundation to a successful, long-lasting fat-loss program. However, certain nutritional supplements, when used properly, can be helpful in supporting your program. Below are my top recommended supplements to aid fat loss.

Conjugated Linoleic Acid (Tonalin®)

Conjugated linoleic acid (CLA) is a naturally occurring fatty acid found most abundantly in beef and dairy fats. Research has found that supplements of CLA can be helpful in reducing body fat while maintaining or increasing lean muscle mass. Specifically CLA acts to stimulate the breakdown of stored fat in the fat cells, reduce the number of existing fat cells, and prevent fat storage.

In a recent clinical trial, overweight subjects taking Tonalin® CLA for one year, without changing their diet and exercise habits, had a 9% reduction in body fat and a 2% increase in lean body mass compared to the placebo group.6

Several additional studies lasting from 4 weeks to 6 months have shown that Tonalin® CLA is effective in reducing body fat compared to placebo groups. Based on the clinical studies, the recommended dosage of Tonalin® CLA is 3.4 grams per day. The product is very well tolerated. No significant adverse events have been reported.

Green Tea

As one of the most popular beverages consumed worldwide, green tea is known for its benefits for heart health, cancer protection, weight loss, and much more

Green tea contains a number of beneficial compounds including volatile oils, vitamins, minerals, caffeine, and potent antioxidants called polyphenols. Research has shown that green tea can facilitate weight loss by increasing thermogenesis - the rate at which the body burns calories. This was initially attributed to its caffeine content, however recent studies have shown that this is due to an interaction between its high content of polyphenols, specifically the catechin epigallocatechin gallate (EGCG) along with caffeine.7-9

Most studies documenting the health benefits of green tea have involved 3 to 10 cups per day. Tablets and capsules are available. Look for a product that is standardized for total polyphenol content and/or catechin concentrations. Most products provide 60% to 97% polyphenols and/or EGCG.

There are no serious side effects known, even with intakes of as much as 20 cups per day. Since it contains some caffeine, higher doses may cause restlessness, insomnia, and increased heart rate.

Hydroxycitric Acid

Hydroxycitric acid (HCA) is a compound derived from the fruit Garcinia cambogia, which is native to South and Southeast Asia. HCA has been popular as a weight loss supplement for years. It appears that HCA supports weight loss by reducing appetite, enhancing the breakdown of fat and inhibiting fat storage without affecting the central nervous system. There may be other benefits as well as newer research has found that it can reduce cholesterol and triglycerides.

No serious side effects have been reported with HCA. While earlier studies found benefits in dosages around 1200 to 1500 mg HCA daily, newer research supports greater benefits at a higher dosage, such as 2800 mg per day.

Phase 2® ® Standardized White Kidney Bean Extract

Phase 2® ® is an extract of the white kidney bean that promotes fat loss by temporarily neutralizing starches from the diet. It inhibits the action of an enzyme called alpha-amylase - the enzyme responsible for breaking down starches into sugar. Foods high in starch include bread, pasta, potatoes, rice, and baked goods. Over-consumption of these foods (larger portion sizes) and physical inactivity can lead to weight gain. In several clinical studies Phases 2® has been shown to reduce the amount of sugar absorbed from starchy meals and promote fat loss.

Measuring Success

Keep in mind that the bathroom scale only tells you how much you weigh. It does not tell you what your body composition is, or whether you are carrying excess fat. In fact, if you are exercising, losing body fat and gaining lean muscle mass it is possible that you may notice either no change in the scale or even a slight increase in weight initially. While you will be improving your level of fitness, your total body weight may not change. Weighing yourself on a scale tells you very little about your health and should not be relied upon as a measure of success.

Here are some simple/easy ways to measure your progress and success:

· Look in the mirror - take an honest look at your body in the mirror. As you lose body fat and gain lean muscle you will notice your shape change. Your muscles will become more prominent and there will be less flabby areas.

· Evaluate how you look and feel - as you lose body fat you will feel lighter, have more energy and generally feel better about yourself.

· Judge how your clothes fit - as you lose body fat you will notice that your clothes feel more loose and fit better.

· Check your percentage of body fat - using the above-mentioned methods.

Carrying excess body fat is a known risk factor for many chronic health problems, such as heart disease, cancer and diabetes, and psychological issues. Knowing your percentage of body fat is the best way to determine if you are at risk. To achieve a healthy body composition, proper diet and regular exercise are essential. Nutritional supplements such as CLA, green tea, hydroxy citric acid and Phase 2® can provide a supportive role by reducing body fat storage, enhancing fat breakdown, boosting metabolism and neutralizing starches. Monitoring body fat levels with the above mentioned methods will help to guide progress and keep you on track in maintaining a lean body.

Muscle building and fat loss

People go to the gym and exercise regularly for two main reasons - building muscle mass, and losing fat. The detailed exercise and nutrition plans that your trainer chalks out for you are built with these specific purposes in mind. In most cases, this is a simultaneous activity, as you burn more fat, your muscles get developed. And the more muscles that you have developed in your body, the easier it will be for you to burn fat in the future. Gaining muscle but not losing fat is a result that many people have noticed in their time though, and this has them perplexed and confused.

First and foremost, you must know if it is possible to gain muscle and lose fat at the same time. The answer is no, this is not possible. The human body cannot perform both these tasks at the same time, though ideally everyone would be absolutely delighted if this were the case. As a result, many people start panicking when they begin to notice that they are not losing fat.

Everybody who goes to the gym has a particular purpose in mind. Some are there to solely get rid of fat, whereas some are focused primarily on building muscle. Everyone would love to achieve both these results simultaneously, but sadly this is not the case. Seasoned and experienced gym visitors are well aware of this, and as a result plan their exercise routines in a balanced manner. They know how to gain muscle without losing weight, and know how to go about fat burning as well.

The Reasoning

The reason is the process of anabolism. Anabolism refers to the requirement of the human body to have a supply of more calories than those that are expended, in order to build muscle mass. This is one of the fundamental tips to gain muscle fast. This can only be effective if the body is receiving more calories than it is releasing.

On the other hand, the process of losing weight or burning fat requires the human body to burn more calories than it is receiving. The contradiction between the two processes is the reason that people find that they are gaining weight in terms of muscle but not losing any body fat. The human body only knows how to gain muscle without losing weight.

Carefully analyzes the processes of losing weight and gaining muscle separately. Losing weight requires you to do more cardiovascular exercises, consume a low-fat, low carbohydrates, and low calories diet. Conversely, for building muscle, you need to do absolutely no cardiovascular exercises, eat a diet high in carbohydrates, calories, and proteins, and of course, lift weights. Both the processes are completely contradictory to each other, so obviously the end result is that people will have the same amount of fat, or they will be losing fat but not gaining weight. This is also why many people fail to see results in their exercise regimen, and as a result they just give up.

The Solution

There is a possible solution to this contradictory situation for you. First, of all, you need to accept that you cannot lose fat and build muscle at the same time. You need to alter your exercise regime and focus on both goals separately. Dividing your exercise plan into phases will be a solution that will help. One way for you to go about this is by dividing your phases based on the season. Winter season is a good time to bulk up your muscles and focus on gaining muscle, as the extra fat on your body will be welcome. In the summer season, you can focus on burning up the excess fat and develop a leaner look.

Eating a proper and healthy diet will also aid you in this process. You need to reduce the amount of dietary fat that enters your system. This adds up in an increase in your body's rate of metabolism. Having an increased rate of metabolism helps you to gain muscle quicker, and also enables you to lose fat more efficiently. Increase the consumption of vegetables, and decrease the consumption of foods rich in starch as well.

It should not discourage you from visiting the gym, and it should not leave you feeling frustrated or depressed. You need to understand how your body works, set goals for yourself, and then work hard to achieve it. Time and patience will give you the required results that you wish for.

CHAPTER 7- WHAT ARE GOOD FATS- LIST OF LOW-FAT FOODS

Fat in general, is one of the three classes of foods called macronutrients (the others are protein and carbohydrates). All foods containing fat - even pure oils - contain a mixture of three kinds of fat - saturated, polyunsaturated and monosaturated. Fats are commonly classified as good fats and bad fats.

What are good fats & bad fats?

Good fats are all fats which are naturally found in foods; they are not heat processed and are therefore not damaged. Especially important good fats are the essential omega-3's, but any fat that's normally found in food- like avocados, eggs, flaxseed, olives, coconut and nuts can be a good fat when consumed in a healthy diet.

Bad fats are damaged fats. They include oils that have been used and reused in frying. Bad fats are hydrogenated oils, also known as "trans-fats."

Why do I need good fats?

Good fats are absolutely essential for human health. They provide the building blocks for many important hormones and structures in the human body. Omega-3 fatty acids are a great example of a healthy fat, as they are the building blocks of anti-inflammatory hormones.

Why should I avoid bad fats?

Bad fats or trans fats are often used in packaged goods such as chips, pretzels, cookies, fast food, shortenings and some margarine brands. They are even found in some brands of peanut butter. Because the body can't break them down, trans fats (or bad fats) attach to the arteries and may result in plaque formation, which can be linked to heart disease, diabetes, breast cancer and asthma, as well as other illnesses.

How much good fat do I need?

Good question. Native hunter and gatherer societies have thrived on diets with a wide range of fat intake. Most experts suggest approximately 30% of calories as a dietary goal for good fats, which should come from a good mix of naturally occurring saturated, polyunsaturated, and monounsaturated fats. – however, the percentage will ultimately depend on your individual level of carb consumption.

List of low fat foods

The problem of obesity has attained a global status. Sedentary and unhealthy lifestyle has aggravated the problem even more. Nonetheless, more and more people are becoming conscious of their weights and are trying to look out for ways to control their weights. Proper diet and regular exercises are the best ways to keep your weight within limits. Low fat foods go a long way in reducing your weight. However, to incorporate these foods in your daily diet, you must know which are the foods with low fat content. In this book, I have provided a extensive list of low-fat foods across different categories for your reference.

Fruits

Fresh fruits often constitute a healthy and nutritious diet. However, if you are planning to eat fruits as a part of your weight control diet, then you must eat only those fruits that are low in fats. Not all fruits are low in fat content. Here is low fat food list of fruits and berries.

- Apple
- Apricot
- Avocado
- Banana
- Cantaloupe
- Casaba melon
- Fig
- Grape
- Grapefruit
- Honeydew melon
- Lemon
- Lime
- Kiwi
- Mango
- Orange
- Papaya
- Peach
- Pear
- Persimmon
- Pineapple
- Plums
- Pomegranate

- Tangerine
- Watermelon
- Blueberries
- Cherries
- Cranberries
- Currants
- Gooseberries
- Loganberries
- Raspberries
- Strawberries

Vegetables

Most of the vegetables cannot be eaten raw or consumed as juices. Hence, their cooking method is important in determining their fat content. Vegetables should always be cooked in minimal cooking oil to extract maximum benefit from them. Low fat vegetables include:

- Acorn squash
- Artichoke
- Asparagus
- Bean sprouts
- Beets
- Brussels sprouts
- Butternut squash
- Cabbage
- Cauliflower
- Carrots

- Celery
- Corn
- Cucumbers
- Eggplant
- Green beans
- Hubbard squash
- Iceberg lettuce
- Leeks
- Mushrooms
- Onions
- Parsnips
- Potatoes(Baked)
- Rutabaga
- Sweet potatoes
- Tomatoes
- Turnips
- Wax beans
- Zucchini
- Bok choi
- Broccoli
- Collard Greens
- Kale
- Mesclun
- Mustard Greens
- Romaine Lettuce
- Spinach

- Water Crest
- Beet Greens
- Chard etc.

Meat and Fish

Similar to vegetables, meat and fish should also be cooked in less oil. Besides, they should be consumed only in the correct forms, such as, skinless or in lean forms only. Following are low fat meats and fish varieties.

- Egg whites
- Chicken breast (skinless)
- Turkey breast (skinless)
- Lean beef
- Lean pork
- Lean lamb
- Lean veal
- Liver
- Rabbit
- Venison
- Game hens
- Game birds
- Catfish
- Cod
- Flounder
- Haddock
- Halibut

- Herring
- Mackerel
- Pollock
- Salmon
- Sea bass
- Snapper
- Swordfish
- Trout
- Tuna
- Clams
- Crab
- Crayfish
- Lobster
- Mussels
- Octopus
- Oysters
- Scallops
- Squid
- Shrimp

Legumes

Most of the legumes are very high in proteins and low in fats. Legumes gives you the required energy without being too high in fat content.

- Black beans
- Black-eyed peas
- Chickpeas

- Great northern beans
- Green peas
- Kidney beans
- Lentils
- Lima beans
- Mung beans
- Navy beans
- Pinto beans
- Soy beans
- Split peas
- White beans
- Adzuki beans

Bread and Grains

Bread and grains constitute the most important part of your diet. Hence, knowing which grains are low in fat, can help you to incorporate them in your daily diet and thus help reduce weight. Low fat foods in this category include:

- Whole wheat bread
- Bulgur
- Cracked wheat
- Oatmeal
- Whole Grain Cornmeal
- Brown Rice
- Wild Rice
- Millet

- Quinoa
- Sorghum
- Triticale
- Whole wheat flakes
- Whole wheat buns
- Whole wheat rolls
- Muesli
- Whole grain barley
- Pearl barley
- Whole rye
- Whole wheat crackers
- Whole wheat pretzels
- Whole wheat pasta
- Whole wheat tortillas
- Brown rice pasta
- Quinoa pasta

Dairy Products

Although dairy products are often said to be rich in fats, their low fat versions can be consumed even if you are on a weight loss diet. These include:

- Milk - 1% reduced fat
- Skimmed milk
- Low fat goat's milk
- Soy milk
- Low fat yogurt
- Low fat cheese

- Goat cheese
- Skimmed mozzarella
- Low fat string cheese
- Neufchatel cheese
- Low fat cream cheese

The foods mentioned in the above list should be consumed in fresh and recommended form only. This is the best way to gain maximum benefit from them.

CHAPTER 8- BODY FAT SCALE- HOW TO MEASURE THE BODY FAT

With the increasing awareness about obesity and diseases related to this condition, more and more people are thronging the gyms, or trying other weight loss methods. It is very easy to determine your body mass index and relate the findings to evaluate your weight. You just have to do some calculations based on a given formula and interpret the result as per the BMI chart. The four categories as per the BMI chart are: underweight, normal weight, overweight, and obese. You can find out the category to which you belong, as per your score. However, it is not possible to find out the percentage of body fat, using the BMI chart. A body fat scale is useful for this purpose.

Ways to Measure Body Fat

The most common tools and methods that are used for measuring the body fat are, Near Infrared Interactance (NIR), Dual Energy X-ray absorptiometry (DXA), calipers (skinfold measurements), and hydrostatic (underwater) weighing. NIR is based on infrared spectroscopy, and the percentage of body fat is calculated on the basis of resultant figures. DEXA is basically a scanning tool to determine the bone density, but it is also useful for determining the level of body fat. Calipers measure body fat, according to the skin fold thickness, at various sites, like the abdomen and chest. Hydrostatic weighing is based on the principle that a person with a low body fat weighs more under water, and vice-versa.

All these body fat monitoring tools have many disadvantages. While the results of NIR and calipers are not considered accurate; DEXA and underwater weighing are very much expensive, and may not be available everywhere. Nevertheless, DEXA, and underwater weighing are considered the most accurate methods of measuring of body fat. Despite being accurate, these tools are not commonly in use, due to their high costs.

Body Fat Scale

Nowadays, body fat scales are commonly used for measuring and monitoring body fat percentage. These scales use a technique called Bioelectrical Impedance Analysis (BIA). Use of this tool involves circulation of a low level of electric current through the body. A electric current can pass easily through muscles that contain fluids, whereas fat tissues show some resistance. More resistance to the electric current means the presence of more fat tissues and vice-versa. The speed of the passage of current through the body is calculated, to determine the density of the body fat; which is then interpreted in conjunction with other factors, like the weight and height, to evaluate the body fat percentage. While some advanced body scales can calculate the final figure on their own; others provide values that have to be interpreted.

Pros and Cons

The speed of passage of electric current can be influenced by many factors, like amount of water in the body, temperature of the body, and recent physical activity. So, there are doubts regarding the accuracy of the results. Factors like age, gender, and race, are not taken into account. Even though some of the scales can automatically consider these factors, the results are only rough estimates.

However, the advantage of this tool is its easy availability, as compared to others, like DEXA,and hydrostatic weighing. Body fat scales are cheaper too. Once bought, they can be used regularly.

Tips for Optimum Use

- In order to get accurate results from a body fat scale, you must know how to use it in a proper way.
- Don't compare your results with that of your friends. Compare the results with your own standards, and measure your progress regularly.
- Always remember to adjust the machine according to your profile.
- Try to use the scale at the same time everyday. If possible, use the machine at the same room temperature, every day.
- Avoid physical activities and water consumption, before the test. Clean the footpads before using the scale.
- Always try to buy the best among those available in the market. The expensive ones are likely to be more efficient.
- If needed, you can purchase scales with multiple user memory. Some models can store profiles of more than ten people.
- You can compare the results of the scale, with other tools, like calipers.
- In short, body fat scales are easily accessible devices to determine the body fat percentage. If used in the proper way, they can be of great help in monitoring the fat content of your body.

CHAPTER 9- HOW TO REMOVE STOMACH FAT

Everyone prefers to have a flat stomach. In addition to the unpleasant appearance resulted from excess belly fats, it may pose serious health conditions. Belly fat increases the risk of inflammation and hardening of blood vessels. Considering this, people having accumulated fats in the midsection for a prolonged duration are at a higher risk of developing diabetes, cardiovascular diseases and heart problems. Hence, it is very essential to lose stomach fats.

The chances of developing belly fats are more in people who indulge on eating excess fatty foods and drinking beers. Generally, women, following their pregnancy, tend to put on more belly fats. As far as the best ways to remove fat are concerned, there are no magic tips as such. Experts say that a specific diet plan or a particular exercise is not effective to target belly fats only. On the brighter side, stomach fats are the first to get rid of while losing weight.

How to Get Rid of Stomach Fat

As per statistics, about 99 percent of individuals who have lost weight successfully, lose stomach fat prior to losing fats in the other body parts. Also, it is observed that the upper body part loses more weight in comparison to the lower portion. It is due to the fact that the type of fat in the waistline is visceral fat, which is easier to lose than the fats located under the skin (subcutaneous fat). Hence, with proper ways for fat removing, one can sport a flat stomach.

Cook Your Own Food

Those who want to get rid of stomach fat are often attracted towards fad diets or crash diets. But remember, they are good for short-term results. Moreover, these diet plans can cause a deficiency of important nutrients and can lead to several health problems. To lose tummy fat fast, you should follow a balanced and healthy diet. Your diet should be high in protein and fibers, moderate in carbohydrates and low in fats and sodium. Make a habit of cooking your food in less oil. Avoid overeating or over-consumption of calories. Your meals should include foods that burn fats, for example, apples, citrus fruits, chilies, pulses, cinnamon, cucumbers, ginger, asparagus, and tomatoes. Including home-made food in your diet can help control the daily calorie intake.

Include Whole Grains in Your Diet

One of the best ways for removing stomach fat is adding adequate amounts of whole grain foods in the diet plan, rather than consuming refined grains. Studies have been conducted on people who consumed the same diet, but with different grain servings. In one group whole grains were given with fruits, vegetables, and other food items; whereas the same diet with refined grains was served in another group. The outcome is that participants consuming whole grains lose belly fat more than the others.

Change Eating Habits

In addition to the foods that are included in the diet plan, what is equally important is the timing and frequency of eating. No doubt, serving a large meal at a time is the key factor for gaining excess fat. The logic behind this is that the body does not get time to covert the fats into energy. In order to avoid such a condition, you can consume less servings frequently. Instead of 2 large meals, you can have 4-5 smaller meals per day. This will speed up your metabolism. Your body will burn more calories and store less fat. Having 4-5 meals during a day will keep you satiated and help you stay away from junk food. Reduce the intake of sugar, sugary drinks and alcoholic drinks. Incorporate low glycemic fruits and vegetables, nuts, lean protein foods, whole grain cereals, beans, legumes, fish, low-fat versions of dairy products and small amounts of healthy fats (like olive oil) in your regular diet. Drink lots of water, at least 8 to 10 glasses, in a day. Water is essential for the health of the cells. It aids in digestion. It works as a detoxifying agent and as an appetite suppressant. Do not skip your meals and have a heavy breakfast.

Exercise to Lose Stomach Fat

In contrast to many people's views about removing stomach fat, spot exercise is not effective for getting rid of belly fats. Even if you perform several rounds of crunches or abdominal exercise daily, you are not going to flatten your stomach. Nevertheless, you can strengthen and tone the abdominal muscles with spot exercise. While speaking about the exercises to lose belly fat, performing moderate physical activities for about 45-50 minutes, 4 to 6 times a week, is sufficient to effectively remove fat from stomach. The more time you indulge on rigorous cardio exercise (like brisk walking, cycling, running, jogging, etc.) and aerobic exercise, the faster you will lose belly fats. Remember, skipping few days in between will only mean you start all over again. You can increase the duration and intensity of the exercise gradually, as your stamina increases. Do not forget to perform 5-10 minutes warm-up exercises before you begin with your exercise regime.

Be active and avoid use of locomotives for short distances. Prefer taking the stairs instead of using the elevator. Walk as much as you can and avoid driving your vehicle for short distances. Avoid late night dinners and heavy food at night. You should enjoy your dinner 2-3 hours before going to bed. There are certain lifestyle changes that can indirectly help you to lose tummy fat. Avoid excessive consumption of alcohol. Stop smoking and avoid taking too many medications. You should stay away from all those things which lead to hormone imbalance and obesity. Yoga, meditation, music, leisurely walk, sports activities, vacations, sufficient sleep, etc. help lower stress, an unavoidable factor of modern life. Excessive stress can result in hormonal imbalance and obesity. So, leading a stress-free lifestyle is important, if you want to shed those extra pounds.

Last but not the least, the best way to lose belly fat is to follow the above tips from today itself. Many times, we tend to postpone things until the day comes, when it is too late to correct. Be patient and inculcate healthy lifestyle changes to lose stomach fats effectively. Losing stomach fats not only improves your appearance and general health, but you will also become more confident with yourself.

Exercises that reduces stomach fat

A sedentary lifestyle is belly fat's best friend. Sitting promotes belly fat, and that is something we all need to work towards, and change. The bad stuff around the waist can only be removed, or lessened, when you get up and move.

If you cannot invest a lot of time at the gym, just 3 hours a week of aerobic exercises can do the trick. Engage in activities such as walking, jogging, cycling, swimming, etc.; working out at an up tempo can really make a difference.

The key to being consistent is including a variety of exercises to keep yourself motivated. As soon as the workouts begin to seem tedious or mundane, change it immediately to keep it fun

STEP- HOP

- Stand with your feet hip-width apart.
- Keep your knees slightly bent, with both hands on the side.
- You can even keep your hands on the hips for more support.
- Step forward with your right foot, and lift the left knee till the hip level as you hop on the right leg.
- You need to hop straight up in such a way that you are almost jogging or marching in place.
- Bring your right leg back to the floor; bring both the feet together.
- Do at least 15—20 reps on both legs, as you alternate sides.
- COBRA POSE
- To do this yoga pose, lie on your stomach with the legs spaced out and the toes touching the floor.
- Keep your palms underneath your shoulders and take a deep breath.
- While inhaling, lift your chest and head off the floor to look up toward the ceiling.
- Hold your buttocks firm, and push your pelvis down toward the floor.
- Bend backwards as far as you can without hurting yourself.
- Breathe normally, and hold the position for 15—30 seconds.
- Exhale, and slowly come back down to return to the starting position. Stretch your arms in front of you.
- Relax for 15 seconds and do the pose for 10 times to begin with. Once you are comfortable, gradually increase it to 30 times.

PLANK

- Place a mat on the floor, and kneel on all fours with your hands underneath the shoulders.
- Stretch both legs one at a time at the back to come into the plank position.
- Make sure that the position is long and straight. This means, no lifting the buttocks in the air, or sagging the hips.
- Press your hands as firmly as you can on the mat and your heels backward; make sure you are comfortable throughout the exercise.
- Hold the position for 1—2 minutes, and then come down on all fours.

LUNGE TWIST

- Stand with your feet hip-width apart.
- Put both hands over the hips and lunge forward with the right leg.
- As you bend forward, make sure your knee is over the ankle.
- Rotate your torso and arms to the right side, and hold the position for a second or two.
- Rotate back to the center, and push off with your right foot to come back to the starting position.
- Do at least 15—20 reps on both legs, as you alternate sides.

BOWL POSE

- Lie on your stomach on a mat and keep your legs together while your hands are resting on either side of your body.
- Inhale, and while exhaling, bend your knees and bring it closer to your buttocks.
- Lift your head slightly and bend backward from your waist.
- Hold your ankles with your hands and lift your knees as high as you can.
- Keep breathing normally, and hold the position for 15—30 seconds.
- Exhale and slowly come back to the starting position.
- Relax for 15 seconds and do the pose for 10 times to begin with. Once you are comfortable, gradually increase it to 30 times.

BICYCLE CRUNCHES

- Lie flat on the floor with your lower back pressed toward the floor.
- Place your hands at the back of your head and lift your knees to about a 45° angle.
- Slowly begin a bicycle pedal motion and alternate touching your elbows to the opposite knees.
- As you twist back and forth, make sure you are breathing evenly.
- One complete circle with both legs will be counted as 1 rep.
- Do at least 3 sets of 15 reps for 2—3 times a week.

BOAT POSE

- Lie down on the mat, stretch your legs, and face the toes toward the ceiling.
- Keep your arms on either side of your body, with palms flat on the floor.
- Inhale, and while exhaling, lift your head, chest, and legs off the floor.
- Stretch your arms out, and keep it parallel to the floor. If the pose is too difficult for you, hold the inside of your knees for support.
- Breathe normally, and hold the position for 30—60 seconds.
- Relax for 15 seconds and do the pose for 5 times to begin with. Once you are comfortable, gradually increase it to 30 times.

PLANK TWIST

- Kneel on all fours and get into the plank position (mentioned above).
- Slowly twist your lower body toward the left, and then come back to the center.
- As you do so, lift your leg up and bring it forward to touch your left elbow.
- Inhale, and hold the position for a second. Now exhale, and bring your leg back to the starting position.
- Do the same on the right side. This will be 1 rep. Do at least 3 sets of 10—15 reps for 2—3 times a week.

KETTLEBELL FRONT SQUATS

- Stand with your feet hip-width apart.
- Hold the kettlebell with both hands, and keep it in front of your chest.
- Keep the elbows close to your body, and squat.
- Your legs need to be firm on the floor, while your hips should be pushed back so that the thighs are parallel to the floor.
- Hold this position for a second, and return to the standing position.
- Repeat the squat at least 15—20 times.

CAMEL POSE

- To do this yoga pose, sit on the floor so that your knees are touching it.

- Slowly, lift your upper body and bring your entire body weight on the knees.
- Inhale, and while exhaling, arch your back as far as you possibly can.
- Tilt your head back, and bring your hands behind as you stretch, and try to touch your ankles.
- Breathe normally, and hold the position for at least 20—30 seconds.
- Relax for 15 seconds and do the pose for 5 times to begin with. Once you are comfortable, gradually increase it to 30 times.

HIPS UPS

- Similar to a side plank-hold, you need to lie on your left side on the floor.
- Keep your feet stacked on top of each other, and rest on your elbow.
- Inhale, and while exhaling, raise your hips off the floor.
- At this point, your body should be straight from head to toe.
- Slowly lower your hips and come back to the starting position.
- Do this at least 10—15 reps on both sides.

Foods that cause stomach fat

If your body ever came out with a 'most wanted list of criminals' who are responsible for bloating you out, it would definitely include salt, carbohydrates, and fats as the chief culprits. Now, when I mention carbohydrates and fats, I only point towards some particular types of carbohydrates and fats. It is simple carbohydrates which are easy to digest (such as refined sugars, glucose, fructose, and sucrose), and saturated and trans fats which are the culprits. Along with a list of specific food items that are high in these nutrients, let's understand how these nutri-villains go about in adding that extra inches and pounds to your body.

Saturated and Trans Fats

Fats are an important source of energy for the body. However, the excess fat that is left behind after the body has burned what it needed is what spells trouble. Since these fats have a tendency to harden when stored in room temperature, we can assume that once stored elsewhere on the body, it is usually very difficult to revert to them and burn them as fuel. Most non-vegetarian food sources are high in saturated fats, with some vegetarian fats and oils also being included. Besides being difficult to burn once stashed away, saturated and trans fats bring a malefic package of harmful cholesterols, and these cholesterols eat into the good ones, thereby taking over gradually. The equation is simple—more the quantity of harmful cholesterol, more the person is prone to develop heart disease. No wonder obesity and heart attacks are in perpetual matrimony to each other. Foods high in trans fats include:-

- Fast foods
- Commercially available fried snacks
- Cookies
- Muffins
- Pre-popped popcorn in butter flavor
- Potato fries and wedges
- Snack pies
- Burgers
- Pizzas of commercial pizzerias
- Croissants
- Cupcakes
- Canned or processed food items such as cereal, pasta, soups
- Food mixes
- Packaged sauces

- Restaurant cooked food
- Vegetable shortening
- Frozen food items
- Whole dairy products
- Butter, lard
- Beef, pork, bacon, chicken

Most of the time, it is the presence of partially hydrogenated oils in the preparation of these commercial and processed food items. Partially hydrogenated oils increase the shelf life of these products, therefore, commercial manufacturers generously use it in their products. Trans fats are a type of saturated fats.

Refined Carbohydrates

Refined carbohydrates are easy to digest, and, as such, are a great source of instant energy. However, if consumed in excess, these get converted into fats and get stored away, especially around the abdominal girth. Simple carbohydrate-rich foods such as sweets, desserts, chocolates, cookies, etc., are some of the chief foods that cause belly fat in women, as the femmes are more prone to munch on these delectable edibles on those times when they feel emotionally down or are going through one of those mood swings. Primary foods that fall under this category include:-

- Chocolates
- Candies
- Cookies
- Cakes
- Muffins

- White rice
- Refined flour
- Ice creams
- Coffee/Tea (if refined sugar is used)
- Sweetened beverages and sodas
- Table sugar
- Sugar coated cereals

Basically, any food high in simple carbohydrates such as those containing refined sugar fall under this category.

Salt

Wondering how salt pads you up? Well, sodium molecules fortify the already stored fat cells by surrounding them with water, further puffing them out. This water accumulation manifests as a bloated appearance, and adds to the overall girth, as the excess salt that is left over after the digestive process has concluded passes over the stomach area first, the flourishing ground of the previously stored fats. Most canned, fried, processed, and salted foods contain salt or sodium. Besides these, other foods high in salt or sodium are:-

- Cheese
- Meat
- Cornmeal
- Chickpeas
- Sauces
- Seasonings
- Pickles and chutneys
- Oysters

- Self-raising flour

The next time you're merrily munching away at those ready-made rice krispies, remember that you're inviting the terrible trio—salt, trans fats, and simple carbs in the rice used—into your system at the same time.

Other causes of stomach fat

Major causes are genetics, improper digestion, stress, menopause, slow metabolism, lack of exercise, and excessive eating.

Stress: According to researches, a pot belly can result from stress. When you are under stress, the cortisol hormone is released. Cortisol stimulates the storage of fat around the belly. When you are stressed, you often feel hungry and tend to eat more, which can lead to excessive weight gain.

Genetics: There are 2 body types, namely, apple body and pear body. In case of a pear-shaped body, fat accumulation occurs in the lower parts of the body. Fat stored in the abdomen and middle portion results in the body acquiring an apple shape. Most people have an apple-shaped body. If any of your parents have any such body type, then you are at a higher risk of developing a pot belly.

Slow metabolism: Metabolism rate is a major contributing factor of abdominal fat. A slower metabolism causes less burning of calories and excess accumulation of fats. You can increase the basal metabolic rate (BMR) with the help of a nutritious and balanced diet and regular exercises.

Improper digestion: Overeating and improper digestion can lead to a number of gastrointestinal problems. It causes gas and bloating. Eating late in the night can also interfere with the proper digestion of food. Going to bed immediately after meals also increases the risk of fat storage around the abdominal area.

Lack of exercises: If you follow a lazy lifestyle and keep on eating without any physical activity, then it can lead to obesity and accumulation of abdominal fat. It is extremely essential to burn the calories through exercises to maintain a healthy body weight.

Poor posture: Poor body posture can leave you with a paunch or 'pot belly' appearance. A proper posture creates a great difference in your appearance.

Alcoholism: Alcohol decreases the rate of metabolism and increases obesity. The calories obtained due excess alcoholism are often stored around the abdominal area.

Menopause: Menopause is one of the main reasons of belly fat in women. After menopause, many women tend to accumulate fat around the tummy due to hormonal changes

CHAPTER 10- CONCLUSION

Fat loss represents not only an aesthetic or cosmetic issue but a health imperative as well. Doctors are more and more alarmed about the health dangers associated with obesity, high cholesterol levels and all sorts of ailments resulting from eating junk food. Belly fat is actually deposits of stored energy and they only melt when we burn more calories than we consume.

Fat loss can be achieved by operating the necessary eating habits and starting up a dietary plan that contains only healthy items. Good food is sometimes insufficient if it is not backed up by intense physical work out meant to consume the extra pounds by an acceleration of the metabolism. Some people even turn to all sorts of natural supplements available in a pill form to boost up the body response to physical training and food changes.

Don't expect massive belly fat loss overnight: it takes time, effort, and determination. You could even be tempted to start some crash diet that promises to get you rid of the extra body weight in ten days at the maximum. And here we have to warn against such abuse, because, the body makes strenuous efforts to burn the excessive calories; forcing it to work at a more rapid pace could be detrimental for your health. Moreover, be patient with yourself and don't consider liposuction or higher drug intake as the better alternatives to healthy diets and physical exercises.

Specialists say that the highest success rate for good belly fat loss results from a combination of weight training with abdominal training, aerobic exercises and a healthy diet. Moreover, keep in mind the fact that fat is usually lost systemically and not from just one body part alone. Even if you exercise specific areas like the lower abs or the waist, you could fail in the belly fat loss because the way to approach weight loss is incorrect in the first place. Before muscular training, you'll have to deal with the fat that wraps the tissues by means of aerobic exercises.

The greatest fat burners and friends of belly fat loss include bicycling, walking, jogging, rope jumping and stair climbing. If you manage to work some aerobic exercises for more than thirty minutes, you are likely to achieve great fat loss results. Plus, if you support the training with a diet poor in carbohydrates, but rich in minerals, vitamins, proteins and fibers, belly fat loss will become a very easy to reach goal.

Diet

Your main focus should be on your diet and the foods you eat on a daily basis. The first thing you should do is to eliminate refined sugar and hydrogenated oils. Replace junk and fast food with whole healthy foods. The goal here is to get the most nutritional value from both micro and macro nutrients from the food you consume.

The key is flexibility, so go ahead and build into your diet a day for cheating so food becomes less emotional to you. Take on the point of view that you are energizing your body. In between meals, you should drink green tea because of its anti-oxidant and energy lifting properties not to mention it will save you from grabbing a bag of potato chips.

High Intensity Interval Cardio Training

In order to get maximum fat burn, be sure to incorporate cardio into your workouts. But don't make the mistake of staying on the treadmill for 45 minutes a day. This is not only boring but it is counter productive as your body adapts to the workout and you will experience diminishing returns on your effort.

Instead try HIIT (high intensity interval training) cardio, what you will do instead is spend about 20 minutes on a elliptical alternating between low and high intensity efforts. Your workout should consist of five minute warm up followed by intervals of two minute low intensity and one minute high intensity workouts.

Avoid Spot Training

Most people focus on ab workout with little regard to total fitness. Instead your workout routine should consist of working large muscle groups. This means spending time developing your legs, chest, arms, back and ab muscles.

Not only will you achieve better all round total fitness you will also get more calorie burn for days to come. This is because muscle needs time to repair itself and this increase in your metabolism will cause your body to burn more calories over a period of days.

You can see Quick belly fat loss in a short amount of time by making small changes in your diet and workout routines.

The end

Made in the USA
Monee, IL
11 February 2022